# Cuban Heritage

## Celebrating Diversity in My Classroom

By Tamra B. Orr

*21st Century*
**Junior** Library

**CHERRY LAKE** Publishing

Published in the United States of America by
**Cherry Lake Publishing**
Ann Arbor, Michigan
www.cherrylakepublishing.com

Reading Adviser: Marla Conn MS, Ed., Literacy specialist, Read-Ability, Inc.

Photo Credits: © Roxana Gonzalez / Shutterstock Images, cover; © gg-foto / Shutterstock Images, 4; © Stefano Ember / Shutterstock Images, 6; © Kobby Dagan / Shutterstock Images, 8; © Salvador Aznar / Shutterstock Images, 10; © Felix Lipov / Shutterstock Images, 12; © Stefanie Metzger / Shutterstock Images, 14; © DayOwl / Shutterstock Images, 16; © Marco Crupi / Shutterstock Images, 18; © jesuschueca / Shutterstock Images, 20

Library of Congress Cataloging-in-Publication Data
Name: Orr, Tamra, author.
Title: Cuban heritage / by Tamra B. Orr.
Description: Ann Arbor : Cherry Lake Publishing, 2018. | Series: Celebrating diversity in my classroom | Includes bibliographical references and index.
Identifiers: LCCN 2017035942 | ISBN 9781534107380 (hardcover) | ISBN 9781534109360 (pdf) | ISBN 9781534108370 (pbk.) | ISBN 9781534120358 (hosted ebook)
Subjects: LCSH: Cuba—Social life and customs—Juvenile literature.
Classification: LCC F1760 .O77 2018 | DDC 972.91—dc23
LC record available at https://lccn.loc.gov/2017035942

Cherry Lake Publishing would like to acknowledge the work of The Partnership for 21st Century Skills.
Please visit *www.p21.org* for more information.

Printed in the United States of America
Corporate Graphics

# CONTENTS

Cuba is about the same size as the state of Pennsylvania.

# Charming Cuba

Cuba is the largest island in the Caribbean Sea. The country is 750 miles (1,207 kilometers) long, but only 60 miles (96 km) wide. More than 11 million people live here. Just over 2 million are in the capital city of Havana.

Many people from Cuba have **emigrated** to other countries. There are more than 1 million **immigrants** from Cuba in the United States! What is their home country like? Read ahead to find out!

The Plaze Vieja in Havana was built in 1559.

# Hola Yuma! Que bola?

Do you know any Spanish? If not, you will soon! *"Hola Yuma! Que bola?"* means "Hello American! What's going on?" The people of Cuba all speak Spanish. They often throw in a few Cuban **slang** words. These make the language slightly different than the Spanish spoken in other countries.

Spanish is not the only language Cubans speak. English is commonly used in

The Cuban rumba dance is a mix of African and Spanish dances.

businesses like hotels. It's also spoken in other places where **tourists** visit. About 300,000 Cubans speak a language called Haitian-Creole. It came from the nearby island of Haiti. It is based in French. For example, "hello" in French is *bonjour (bohn-ZOUR)*. In Haitian-Creole, it is *bonjou (bohn-JOO)*. Good-bye in French is *au revoir (oh rev-WAH)*. In Haitian-Creole, it is *orevwa (or-ev-WAH)*.

The Havana Cathedral is one of 11 Roman Catholic cathedrals in Cuba.
It was built from blocks of coral.

# At Church and School

Cuba used to have one main religion. It was Roman Catholic. Pope Francis spent three days in Cuba in 2015. He visited people in several cities. Thousands came out to hear him speak.

Today, only about half of Cubans say they are Catholic. Most others say they are "non-religious." This means they do not follow any religion. A small number of Cubans follow other religions. One is Santeria, an African religion. Followers believe in spirits.

All school is free in Cuba—including college.

Education is very important to Cubans! Children must go to school from ages 6 through 15. All students wear uniforms. Its color tells everyone what grade the child is in. All Cubans know how to read. Cuba has more than 60 universities and 14 medical schools. It has more doctors than almost anywhere in the world. Other countries often turn to Cuba if they need more doctors.

# Ask Questions!

One of the most popular games in Cuba is dominoes. Have you ever played it before? Ask your parents or grandparents if they ever have. Look at the game's rules online. Can you find someone to play dominoes with? How do you like it?

Cubans can enjoy fresh tropical fruit all year long.

# From Plantains to The Cuban

Do you like to share your food? Cubans don't know any other way of eating! Everyone shares both at home and at restaurants. All of the food is brought at the same time. Plates full of black beans, rice, and shredded beef are passed. *Tostones,* or fried **plantains**, are shared, too. *Flan* is a rich pudding with burnt sugar on top. Bowls of it are passed around for dessert.

*Batidos* are milkshakes made with fruit juice.

Have you ever heard of The Cuban sandwich? It is found in many American restaurants today. But it comes from Cuba. Bread is toasted and buttered. Roasted pork and slices of Swiss cheese are put on. They are topped with lots of mustard and dill pickles. The Cuban is often served with extra sweet hot coffee.

Cuban cookbooks are easy to find in the United States. But in Cuba, recipes are not written down. They are handed down with words. Recipes are shared through stories.

The Cuban national baseball team is ranked fifth in the world.

# Baseball and Birds

Can you guess the favorite sport in Cuba? You might think it is soccer. But in Cuba, baseball rules! Everyone loves the game. The country has had some of the best players and teams in the world.

Many bird-watchers love to come to Cuba. The world's tiniest bird is the *zunzuncito*, or bee hummingbird. It lives on the island. It is only 2 inches (5 centimeters) long.

People watch fireworks to welcome in the new year.

More than 100,000 bright pink flamingos also live on the island.

For many years, Americans were not allowed to go to Cuba. President Obama changed that in 2015. People are now reaching out to visit. Everyone is learning that Cuba is full of amazing places and people.

# Look!

Many Cubans do something unusual on New Year's Eve. They do this before the fireworks go off. They toss a bucket of water out the window. They do this to toss out the "old year." Then they can welcome in the new one. Look at this photo. How are these people feeling? What do you do to celebrate the start of a new year?

# GLOSSARY

**emigrated** (EM-ih-grayt-id) left your home country to live in another country

**immigrants** (IM-ih-gruhnts) people who have moved from one country to another and settled there

**plantains** (PLAN-tinz) plants similar to bananas

**slang** (SLANG) colorful word or group of words that often have a different meaning than their original one

**tourists** (TOOR-ists) people who visit a place for fun

## Spanish Words

**batido** (bah-TEE-doh) juice milkshake

**flan** (FLAHN) pudding

**Hola Yuma** (OH-la YOO-mah!) Hello American

**Que bola?** (keh BOH-lah) What's going on?

**tostones** (tohs-TOH-nehs) sliced, fried plantains

**zunzuncito** (zoon-zoon-SEE-toh) bee hummingbird

# FIND OUT MORE

## BOOKS

Ada, Alma Flor. *Island Treasures: Growing Up in Cuba.* New York: Atheneum Books for Young Readers, 2015.

Moon, Walt. *Let's Explore Cuba.* Minneapolis: Lerner Classroom, 2017.

Sheehan, Sean. *Cuba.* New York: Cavendish Square, 2016.

## WEBSITES

### Facts for Kids—Cuba
http://factsforkids.net/cuba-facts-kids-largest-island-caribbean/
Read more facts about the people, economy, and government.

### National Geographic Kids—Cuba
http://kids.nationalgeographic.com/explore/countries/cuba/#cuba-matanzas.jpg
Discover Cuba's people, geography, language, and more.

### Science Kids—Country Facts
www.sciencekids.co.nz/sciencefacts/countries/cuba.html
Read fun facts and enjoy some trivia about the island country.

# INDEX

## ABOUT THE AUTHOR

Tamra Orr is the author of hundreds of books for readers of all ages. She graduated from Ball State University, but moved with her husband and four children to Oregon in 2001. She is a full-time author, and when she isn't researching and writing, she writes letters to friends all over the world. Orr enjoys life in the big city of Portland and feels very lucky to be surrounded by so much diversity.